Polar Bear Facts and Myths

A Science Summary for All Ages

Susan J. Crockford

In science, it matters *what* is right, not *who* is right.

TABLE OF CONTENTS: FACTS & MYTHS

Acknowledgements

Special thanks to editor Hilary Ostrov for checking the details and to friends and colleagues who provided critical feedback and suggestions, especially Cairn Crockford, Kathy Inglis, Jennifer Marohasy, Christopher and Sheran Essex, and young reviewers Moira, Ezri, and Ainsley. Above all, heartfelt thanks to Shar Levine for encouragement and support.

1. Fact or myth? Polar bears are the largest meat-eating animal with four legs.

Fact!

The killer whale or orca is a much larger carnivore, or meat-eater, but it has no legs.

The front feet of the largest polar bears – adult males – are as big as a dinner plate. Big hairy feet are perfect for walking on snow and ice.

Brown bears are the closest relative to polar bears, but they have less hair on the bottom of their feet and longer claws. Grizzly bear is another name for brown bear – they are the same animal.

Female polar bears are about half the size of male polar bears.

If a big polar bear stood up on a basketball court, he would be as tall as the hoop (about 10 feet or 3 meters tall).

A male polar bear has a head as big as the steering wheel of a car. Its front legs are enormous compared to a man's arms.

This big bear was given a drug to make him sleep so he could be weighed and measured – he is not dead. He weighed 1400 pounds (about 645 kilograms). The largest polar bear ever measured weighed 2,200 pounds (1000 kilograms) and stood 11 feet tall (3.4 meters).

2. Fact or Myth? Polar bears live only in the Arctic.

Fact!

The Arctic is here, at the top of the world!

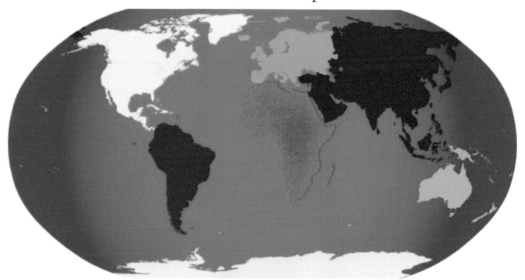

There are no polar bears at the bottom of the world, in Antarctica, where it is also very cold. The Antarctic is where penguins live.

When the Arctic seas are covered by ice in the winter, the area where polar bears live stretches from one side of the world to the other.

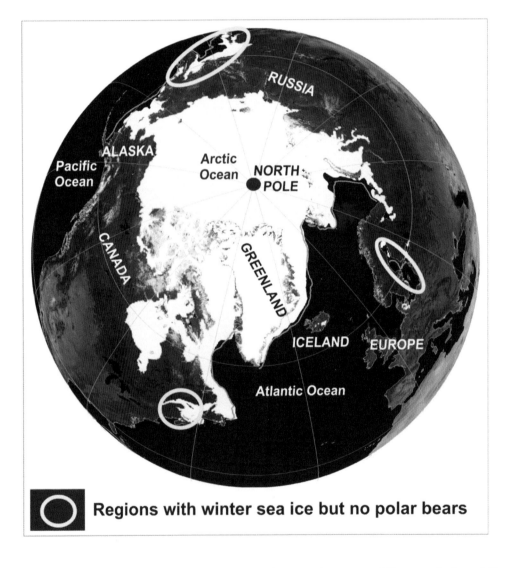

Regions with winter sea ice but no polar bears

This map looks down on the Arctic from the top, like a globe. The North Pole is the furthest north point on Earth – the top of the world. Three areas (circled in yellow) have ice in winter but no polar bears.

3. Fact or Myth? Polar bears live on sea ice near the North Pole.

Myth!

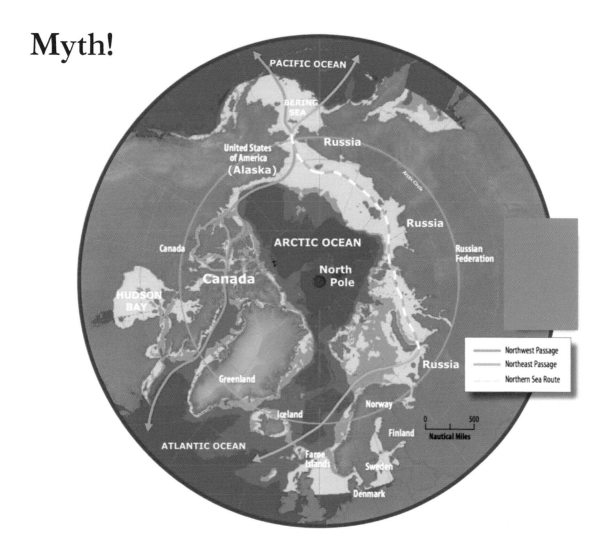

Polar bears live on ice around the edge of the Arctic, mostly in the light blue areas on this map. Very few bears live near the North Pole year round, but many more might visit over the summer.

Sea ice is a frozen crust on top of the ocean, but it is not like a big skating rink or even a frozen pond.

In many places, sea ice is a rough surface that looks like snow covered rocks and mountains.

As the sea ice floating on top of the ocean moves around, it cracks and folds over itself, making huge jumbled blocks of ice with jagged edges. These blocks of ice quickly freeze into solid mountains and ridges.

Polar bears get a lot of exercise climbing over this rough ice and this helps keep them strong.

4. Fact or Myth? Sea ice is a good place to live because it doesn't change.

Myth!

The Arctic is a huge region that is covered in ice over the winter and spring. But every spring and summer, the ice melts and the area that is covered in ice gets smaller. All of the ice gets thinner during the summer, but some of it is so thick it never melts completely.

Then, in the fall, the area of ice grows again as the sea re-freezes. Year after year, sea ice changes with the seasons – as it has always done.

At the end of the cold Arctic winter, new sea ice can be 6-9 feet thick (2-3 meters) but old ice is much thicker – more than 15 feet thick (5 meters).

Over the winter, when it's very cold day after day, the newly-frozen sea ice gets thicker and thicker. In some places, it drifts further south.

The sea ice also gets covered in snow, which provides shelter from the cold and wind for polar bears. Some mothers give birth to their cubs in snow caves on the sea ice.

5. Fact or Myth? Polar bears need really thick sea ice to survive.

Myth!

Polar bears can walk on ice that's only 3 or 4 inches thick (about 10 centimeters). This is how thick the newly-frozen sea ice is in the fall. Polar bears start hunting in the fall as soon as the ice is strong enough to hold them without breaking.

Polar bears find out if newly-frozen or melting ice is strong enough to hold their weight by stepping on it with one foot.

This polar bear is testing some newly-frozen ice to see if it's thick enough to walk on without breaking.

It would do the same thing with thin melting ice in the summer.

6. Fact or Myth? Polar bears live on sea ice in all seasons of the year.

Myth!

Some bears do spend their entire lives on sea ice but, during the summer, a lot of bears go on land and wait for the ice to come back in the fall.

So, polar bears need sea ice but they use land sometimes as well.

Polar bears spend most of their time resting when they are on land during the summer, although sometimes they go exploring.

Some pregnant females stay on shore over the winter, where they give birth to their cubs.

This mother bear and her big cub are resting on a beach waiting for the sea ice to start growing again in the fall.

She isn't nursing the cub any longer, but is still teaching it how to hunt and survive.

7. Fact or Myth? Only pregnant polar bears spend all winter in snow caves.

Fact!

In the late fall, a pregnant female digs a den, which is a cave for giving birth. A bear on land will dig a den into the dirt that later gets covered in deep snow. But a bear on sea ice will dig a den into thick snow that later gets covered in more snow. All the other bears – even mothers with older cubs – keep looking for food over the winter.

Polar bear mothers give birth in their snow cave dens to one or two cubs (sometimes three) in the middle of winter, where they all stay until spring.

Polar bear mothers bring their cubs out of the den when they are three to four months old.

The only food these little cubs eat at first is their mother's milk.

8. Fact or Myth? Polar bears eat baby seals.

Fact!

Polar bears need to eat many baby seals to survive. The fatter these baby seals are, the better polar bears like them.

There are several different kinds of seals in the Arctic, but all give birth to their pups on the sea ice in early spring. This means they are all potential food for polar bears. It's sad for the seals but that's life in the Arctic. Without baby seals to eat, polar bears could not survive.

No matter how many seals polar bears eat, there will still be a huge number of seals left.

Polar bears eat a lot of seals, but they don't eat all of them.

There are many millions of seals in the Arctic – far more than all the polar bears in the world could ever eat.

This means there will always be lots of seals that don't get eaten and they will live long, happy lives.

9. Fact or Myth? Polar bears hunt seals from the ice.

Fact!

Polar bears sneak up on seals resting on the ice or catch them when the seals poke their heads up out of the water to breath beside some ice. Young seals are the easiest to catch because they don't move as fast as older ones, and because they don't always watch for danger.

Polar bear cubs learn how to hunt by watching their mothers.

The older cub shown below, on the left, is helping his mother eat the seal she has caught.

As big as this cub is, he will probably not catch seals himself until he has left his mother to live alone on the ice.

That's why cubs stay with their mothers for two to three years.

10. Fact or Myth? Polar bears need to be fat to stay warm.

Myth!

Polar bears need to be fat to survive through months when there is no food, which happens in the summer *and* the winter. Thick fur keeps polar bears warm but so does digging a hole in the snow.

Polar bears are fattest in the early summer, not the middle of winter.

Most polar bears are fattest in early summer, like this mother bear and her cubs. They are skinniest at the end of winter, when it's still very, very cold.

Polar bears live off their stored fat whenever there is little or no food to eat. It's called fasting – and polar bears are really good at it.

11. Fact or Myth? Summer is the most important feeding season for polar bears.

Myth!

Spring is the most important feeding season for polar bears. Polar bears eat far more seals in the spring than they do in any other season of the year (including winter).

Polar bears work hard to eat as many young seals as they can in the early spring before the babies leave the ice to find their own food.

When the baby seals leave the ice (about the middle of May), polar bears can't catch them. Baby seals are safe from polar bears as long as they stay away from the edge of the sea ice.

Once the baby seals are gone, only adult seals like this one spend time on the ice resting. Polar bears may try to kill and eat these older seals but most of the time, the seals are too quick and careful to be caught.

12. Fact or Myth? Polar bears are always looking for food!

Fact!

In the spring, after feeding on lots of baby seals, this fat mother bear and her cubs have come onto a beach in Alaska to check out the bones of a huge bowhead whale that died the year before. They are looking to see if there is anything left on the bones to eat.

Polar bears are curious and will check out anything that might be food.

Polar bears sometimes explore places where people live to see if there is any food to eat. This can happen at any time of the year.

Polar bears looking for food on land are often not really hungry, they are just looking to see if there is any food around. But sometimes, they are very thin and hungry which makes them very dangerous.

Polar bears will kill and eat people (and dogs) if they can catch them.

13. Fact or Myth? Arctic sea ice is melting.

Fact!

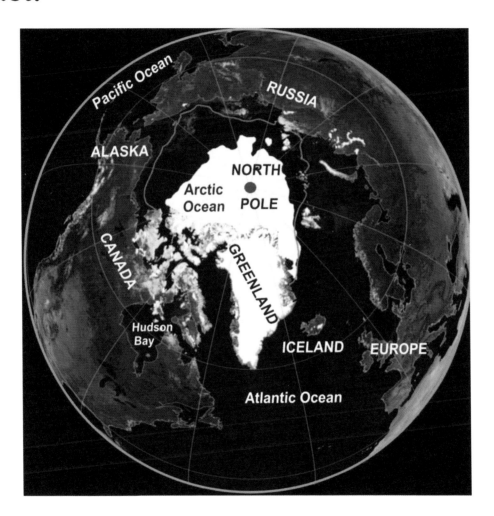

There is much less ice *in summer* now than there was 50 years ago. This map shows what the sea ice has been like in recent years at the end of summer – ice covers only part of the Arctic Ocean instead of most of it, as it did many years ago (compare this to page 8).

When people say that sea ice is melting, they really mean there is less *summer* ice than there used to be and that *summer* ice has more cracks and puddles.

There has been a bit less ice in the fall, winter and spring than there was 50 years ago, but not enough less to hurt polar bears. The amount of sea ice has always changed from year to year but also over larger time periods, like centuries (100 years) and millennia (1,000 years).

A few more cracks and puddles doesn't seem to bothered polar bears.

14. Fact or Myth? Polar bears are good swimmers.

Fact!

Polar bears are excellent swimmers – they can swim a long, long way without resting. Being fat makes polar bears float and their strong front legs and big feet make them fast swimmers.

Polar bear cubs are also good swimmers, except when they are really small.

Very young cubs are not always strong enough for a long swim.

If a mother and her young cub need to cross open water, the cub will sometimes climb up on its mother and sit on her back or shoulders while she swims.

15. Fact or Myth? There are not very many polar bears left in the world.

Myth!

There are many more polar bears in the world now than there were 50 years ago, when so many polar bears had been killed by hunters that people were right to worry about their survival.

But new rules worked to protect the polar bear from too much hunting and at last count (2015), there were as many as 31,000 bears.

Up to 31,000 polar bears living in the Arctic today means they are not close to extinction.

What does 31,000 look like?

A one dollar bill is money but it's also a thin piece of paper that has a standard thickness – every one is the same size.

If you had a one dollar bill for every polar bear and piled all 31,000 of them up, it would make a tower 133 inches tall – more than 11 feet (more than 3 meters).

That's a big stack of paper taller than the biggest polar bear ever measured, standing up on its hind legs – and taller than a basketball hoop.

Up to 31,000 polar bears is a large, healthy population.

16. Fact or Myth? Polar bears will be extinct in the future because of melting sea ice

Myth!

A few years ago, many scientists thought that a lot less sea ice in summer than there was 50 years ago would make thousands of polar bears die. But polar bears have had a lot less ice in summer for more than 10 years – and thousands of them didn't die. Instead, they have done really well – they get fat in the spring and have fat, healthy cubs.

Many scientists still say that thousands of polar bears will die in the future if there is *even less* ice in summer than there is now. But if a lot less ice has not made thousands of polar bears die so far, even less ice is unlikely to do so.

Scientists thought summer sea ice was really important to polar bears, but they were wrong – this means extinction in the future is unlikely.

So far, polar bears have been doing much better than scientists expected with low amounts of sea ice in summer. In some areas, polar bear numbers have gone up.

If ice disappeared in **early spring** sometime in the future, polar bears might have trouble finding enough seals to eat. But there is no sign of early spring ice disappearing – most polar bears still have the sea ice they need to live long, healthy lives.

17. Fact or Myth? Siberian tigers are in more trouble than polar bears.

Fact!

The Siberian tiger is endangered right now – there were only about 480-540 of them counted in 2015. This means there are about 57 polar bears for every single Siberian tiger left in the world.

Polar bears are not rare like Siberian tigers and they don't need the same kind of help to make sure they are still around in the future.

540 Siberian tigers is not very many - a one dollar bill for every Siberian tiger in the world would make a tiny tower of paper just over 2 inches high (about 5 centimeters).

Since there are so few tigers left in Siberia (which is in northern Russia), these big cats might not be saved from extinction in their wild habitat, even with our help.

Some zoos raise families of Siberian tigers just in case wild-born tigers *do* go extinct.

Polar bear families do not need to be raised in zoos to make sure they will be around in the future because there are still so many wild-born polar bears.

18. Fact or Myth: There is no reason to worry about polar bears.

Fact!

It's OK to enjoy watching and learning about polar bears and be happy that the polar bear scientists were wrong about them disappearing. And it's OK not to worry about their future, because polar bears have shown us that they know how to take care of themselves even if sea ice changes.

There will always be good years and bad years for polar bears, but most bears are doing just fine.

There is no good evidence that life is any harder for polar bears now than it was far in the past – the truth is, there are times when living in the Arctic is difficult for some bears.

But the species we call polar bear (*Ursus maritimus*) has lived through periods of time in the past that had much more sea ice than we have today – like the Last Ice Age – and times with much less ice. Polar bears survived all of those past changes in sea ice, so there is no good reason to expect they won't survive future changes as well.

About the author

Susan Crockford has a Ph.D. in Zoology and has studied polar bear ecology and evolution for more than 20 years. She has authored many peer-reviewed papers about different animals (including polar bears) and has been writing a blog on polar bear science since 2012. Her research interests are on past and present aspects of biology and ecology.

Dr. Crockford has also written a short, fully referenced science book about polar bears for adults (*Polar Bears: Outstanding Survivors of Climate Change*) that's filled with useful color images as well as interesting facts.

She is the author of a science-based novel about polar bears called *EATEN* (a polar bear attack thriller) that adults and older teens will enjoy.

Website: www.susancrockford.com

Blog: www.polarbearscience.com

List of Photo Credits

Front cover, Shutterstock, purchased license.
Frontspiece, Shutterstock, purchased license.
Dedication page, Mike Lockhart, USGS, 2005.
Acknowledgements, Shutterstock, purchased license.
Pg 7, Budd Christman, US NOAA, 1982.
Pg 8, Budd Christman, US NOAA, 1982.
Pg 9, Copyright free graphic and Wikipedia Creative Commons license.
Pg 10, US National Snow & Ice Data Service, labels added.
Pg 11, Wikipedia Creative Commons license, labels added.
Pg 12, Eric Regehr, US Fish & Wildlife Service, 2005.
Pg 13, Jessica Robertson, US Geological Survey, 2009.
Pg 14, Steve Amstrup, US Geological Survey, 2001.
Pg 15, Patrick Kelly, US Coast Guard, 2009.
Pg 16, Mario Hoppmann, US NASA, European Geosciences Union.
Pg 17, Shutterstock, purchased license.
Pg 18, Steve Hillebrand, US Fish & Wildlife Service.
Pg 19, US Fish & Wildlife Service.
Pg 20, Shutterstock, purchased license.
Pg 21, Brendan Kelly, US NOAA.
Pg 22, Shutterstock, purchased license.
Pg 23, Suzanne Miller, US Fish & Wildlife Service, 2008.
Pg 24, Shutterstock, purchased license.
Pg 25, US Fish & Wildlife Service, Barrow.
Pg 26, Suzanne Miller, US Fish & Wildlife Service.
Pg 27, Wikipedia Creative Commons license.
Pg 28, Wikipedia Creative Commons license.
Pg 29, US Geological Survey, 2016.
Pg 30, US Fish & Wildlife Service.
Pg 31, US National Snow & Ice Data Service, labels added.
Pg 32, US Geological Survey.
Pg 33, Brian Battaile, US Geological Survey, 2014.
Pg 34, Shutterstock, purchased license.
Pg 35, Brian Battaile, US Geological Survey, 2014.
Pg 36, Wikipedia Creative Commons license.
Pg 37, Gary Kramer, US Fish & Wildlife Service, 2006.
Pg 38, Shutterstock, purchased license.
Pg 39, Wikipedia Creative Commons license.
Pg 40, Wikipedia Creative Commons license.
Pg 41, GoGraphs, purchased license.
Pg 42, Mike Dunn, US NOAA/US Dept. Agriculture.
Pg. 43, Jesse McMillan, commissioned photo.

Made in the USA
Charleston, SC
22 December 2016